Easy Guide to HTML 5

Practical Guide

V. Telman

Copyright © 2024

Practical Guide

1.Introduction to HTML5

What is HTML5?

HTML5, or HyperText Markup Language version 5, is the latest standard for structuring and presenting content on the World Wide Web. It is a markup language that enables web developers to create complex, interactive, and multimedia-rich web applications. HTML5 is designed to be a versatile and robust framework that enhances the capabilities of web pages, allowing for an improved user experience and more dynamic interactions. It is built to support a plethora of features, including rich media handling, native application-like experiences, and seamless integration with other web technologies, such as CSS (Cascading Style Sheets) and JavaScript.

HTML5 is characterized by its simplicity and ease of use. This makes it accessible for developers of all skill levels, from beginners to seasoned professionals. With the evolution of the web, HTML5 has incorporated numerous new features that facilitate a more intuitive approach to web development. HTML5 embraces the modern web's demands by taking user experience to the next level through innovations such as semantic markup, multimedia support, and improved API (Application Programming Interface) capabilities.

History of HTML

The history of HTML can be traced back to the early days of the web itself. HTML was first proposed by Tim Berners-Lee in 1989 while he was working at CERN. The objective was to create a simple way to share and link documents over the internet. The initial version of HTML was relatively basic, consisting of a limited set of tags to format text and create links.

HTML 1.0

The first official version, HTML 1.0, was launched in 1993. It included essential functionalities such as hyperlinks, headings, and lists. As the web community began to grow, so did the need for more complex structures and formatting options.

HTML 2.0

In 1995, HTML 2.0 was released by the Internet Engineering Task Force (IETF). This version standardized various elements and attributes that developers had been using, introducing new elements like forms and tables. However, it still lacked a myriad of features that developers sought to implement in their sites.

HTML 3.2

In 1997, HTML 3.2 emerged, further improving the language with new features like applets and more extensive support for tables and text alignments. It introduced attributes for newer functionalities, making it more versatile, albeit not yet comprehensive enough.

HTML 4.0

The fourth iteration, HTML 4.0, was standardized by the World Wide Web

Consortium (W3C) in 1997. This version provided significant advancements over its predecessors. It brought in the concepts of separation of content and presentation by promoting the use of CSS for styling. HTML 4.0 also included support for internationalization and accessibility, recognizing the web's global audience and the need to accommodate users with disabilities.

XHTML 1.0

As the web continued to evolve, in 2000, XHTML 1.0 was introduced as a reformulation of HTML 4.0 in XML (Extensible Markup Language). XHTML aimed to promote a stricter syntax and adhere to XML standards. It was an attempt to make HTML more robust and future-proof, but its complexity deterred some developers from fully adopting it.

Introducing HTML5

The development of HTML5 began around 2004 as a collaborative project led by the Web Hypertext Application Technology Working

Group (WHATWG). The aim was to create a markup language that would not only include all the features of its predecessors but also address the needs of modern web applications. HTML5 was officially released as a W3C Recommendation in October 2014, marking a significant milestone in the language's evolution.

Features and Benefits of HTML5

HTML5 introduced numerous features and benefits that transformed web development. Here are some of the most notable:

1. Semantic Elements

HTML5 incorporated a variety of semantic elements that improve the structure and readability of web pages. Elements such as `<header>`, `<footer>`, `<article>`, and `<section>` make it easier for developers to define parts of a webpage. This semantic approach enhances accessibility and improves search engine optimization, allowing search engines to better understand the content and context of a webpage.

2. Multimedia Support

One of the major advancements in HTML5 is native support for audio and video content. Elements like `<audio>` and `<video>` allow developers to embed multimedia directly without needing third-party plugins like Flash. This means that web applications can deliver rich media experiences more efficiently, ensuring better performance and improved compatibility across devices.

3. Canvas Element

HTML5 introduced the `<canvas>` element, which enables the dynamic rendering of graphics and animations using JavaScript. This feature is a game-changer for developers, as it allows for the creation of complex games, data visualizations, and interactive graphics without the need for additional libraries or plugins.

4. Forms Enhancements

HTML5 brought many improvements to web

forms, making them easier to use and more user-friendly. New input types such as `email`, `date`, `color`, and `range` enhance form validation and user interaction. HTML5 also introduced attributes like `placeholder`, `required`, and `autofocus`, providing developers with greater control over the user experience.

5. Offline Capabilities

HTML5 has built-in support for offline web applications through the Application Cache API and the newer Service Workers API. These technologies allow web applications to cache resources, enabling users to access them even when they are offline or experiencing a poor internet connection. This functionality is critical for creating reliable applications that can work seamlessly in various environments.

6. Geolocation

HTML5 includes a Geolocation API that allows websites to access the geographical location of a user's device. This feature is essential for location-based services and applications, providing users with personalized experiences, such as localized search results or targeted advertising.

7. Improved API Support

HTML5 introduced robust APIs that allow developers to access additional functionality from within their web applications. For instance, the Drag and Drop API enables users to move items between different parts of a webpage, while the Web Storage API provides a simple way to store data client-side with localStorage and sessionStorage.

8. Enhanced Accessibility

HTML5 focuses on improving accessibility for users with disabilities. By implementing semantic HTML elements and ARIA (Accessible Rich Internet Applications) roles, developers can make their applications more inclusive and usable for everyone. This aligns with the web's mission to serve a diverse audience.

9. Cross-Device Compatibility

HTML5 has been designed with responsive design principles in mind. This means that applications developed using HTML5 can run on various devices, from desktops to tablets and smartphones. The consistent behavior across platforms is essential, given the proliferation of different devices and screen sizes in today's digital landscape.

10. Community and Support

As HTML5 has matured, it has gained wide acceptance and support within the web development community. A vast array of tutorials, libraries, frameworks, and resources are available to assist developers in their projects. Popular frameworks like Angular, React, and Vue.js have been built to harness the power of HTML5, further extending its capabilities.

HTML5 marks a significant advancement in the evolution of web technologies. Its introduction of semantic elements, multimedia capabilities, and improved API support has reshaped how developers create web applications. By simplifying tasks and enhancing user experiences, HTML5 has become a powerful tool that empowers developers to build innovative, responsive, and accessible web applications for today's and tomorrow's digital landscape.

As technology continues to evolve, HTML5 stands as a foundation for the web, poised to adapt and grow to meet the challenges of emerging trends and evolving user needs. Understanding and adopting HTML5 is crucial for developers seeking to stay at the forefront of web development, ensuring they can leverage the latest features and deliver exceptional online experiences.

2. Getting Started with HTML5

HTML5 is the latest version of the HyperText Markup Language (HTML), which is the standard language for creating web pages. HTML5 offers enhanced capabilities for multimedia, graphics, and web application development, making it a vital skill for web developers and designers. This guide provides you with a comprehensive introduction to HTML5, including how to set up your development environment, the basic structure of an HTML5 document, and creating a boilerplate for your projects.

Setting Up the Development Environment

Before you start writing HTML5 code, you need to set up your development environment. Here are the fundamental steps to set up your web development workspace.

1. Choose a Code Editor

A good code editor is essential for writing clean and efficient HTML code. Below are some popular options:

- **Visual Studio Code**: A powerful, feature-rich code editor that supports a wide range of programming languages, including HTML, CSS, and JavaScript. It includes features like syntax highlighting, autocompletion, Git integration, and a vast array of extensions.

- **Sublime Text**: A highly customizable text editor that offers speed and efficiency. With its "Goto Anything" feature and a distraction-free mode, it's great for focusing on code.

- **Atom**: An open-source text editor developed by GitHub. Atom is hackable and includes features like a built-in package manager and collaborative coding through Teletype.

2. Install a Web Browser

You'll need a modern web browser to render and test your HTML5 applications. Popular choices include:

- **Google Chrome**: Widely recognized for its performance and developer tools, which allow you to inspect elements, view console outputs, and debug.

- **Mozilla Firefox**: Known for its user-friendly interface and robust developer tools. Firefox also emphasizes privacy and security.

- **Microsoft Edge**: The newest version of Microsoft's browser includes improvements over its predecessors and integrates tightly with Windows.

- **Safari**: The default browser for macOS and iOS, equipped with tools for web development adapted to Apple devices.

3. Set Up a Local Server (Optional)

For more complex HTML5 projects, especially those that include AJAX and other web technologies, setting up a local server can be beneficial. Software options for creating a local server environment include:

- **XAMPP**: A free, open-source cross-platform web server solution stack package that contains Apache, MySQL, and PHP. It allows you to run your HTML5 applications as if they were on a live server.

- **WAMP**: A similar application to XAMPP, specifically for Windows users. WAMP provides a Windows alternative for web development with Apache as the web server.

- **Live Server extension for Visual Studio Code**: This lightweight solution allows you to run a local server with live reloads directly from your code editor.

4. Directory Structure (Project Organization)

Organizing your project files is crucial for maintaining your HTML5 projects, especially as they grow. A simple directory structure might look like this:

```
my-html5-project/
```

```
├── index.html
├── css/
│   └── styles.css
├── js/
│   └── script.js
└── images/
    └── logo.png
```

In this structure:

- The `index.html` file is the main HTML file.
- The `css` folder contains stylesheets.
- The `js` folder holds JavaScript files.
- The `images` folder stores images used in the project.

Basic Structure of an HTML5 Document

An HTML5 document has a basic structure that includes several essential elements. Below is a breakdown of this structure.

1. The Doctype Declaration

The HTML5 document starts with a `<!DOCTYPE html>` declaration, which informs the web browser that it is to render the document in HTML5.

2. The `<html>` Element

The `<html>` element wraps all other elements of the HTML document. It can have a `lang` attribute to specify the language of the document. For example:

```html
<!DOCTYPE html>
<html lang="en">
```

3. The `<head>` Section

The `<head>` section contains meta-information about the document, such as its title, character encoding, linked stylesheets, and scripts.

Here's an example:

```html
<head>
    <meta charset="UTF-8">
```

```
    <meta name="viewport" 
content="width=device-width, initial-
scale=1.0">
    <title>Your Page Title</title>
    <link rel="stylesheet" 
href="css/styles.css">
    <script src="js/script.js" defer></script>
</head>
```

- The `<meta charset="UTF-8">` tag specifies the character encoding.
- `<meta name="viewport" content="width=device-width, initial-scale=1.0">` sets the viewport size, crucial for responsive design.
- The `<title>` tag sets the title of your document, which appears in the browser title bar or tab.
- Links to external CSS (`<link>`) and JavaScript files (`<script>`) are included.

4. The `<body>` Section

The `<body>` section contains the content of the document, including headings, paragraphs, images, links, and other elements. Here's an example:

```html
<body>
  <header>
    <h1>Welcome to My HTML5 Page</h1>
  </header>

  <main>
    <section>
      <h2>About HTML5</h2>
      <p>HTML5 is a markup language used for structuring and presenting content on the web.</p>
    </section>

    <section>
      <h2>Features of HTML5</h2>
      <ul>
        <li>New semantic elements</li>
        <li>Support for audio and video</li>
        <li>Canvas element for graphics</li>
        <li>Improved form controls</li>
      </ul>
```

```
    </section>
  </main>

  <footer>
    <p>&copy; 2023 Your Name. All rights reserved.</p>
  </footer>
</body>
```

5. Complete HTML5 Document Structure

Below is a complete example of a simple HTML5 document:

```html
<!DOCTYPE html>
<html lang="en">
<head>
    <meta charset="UTF-8">
    <meta name="viewport" content="width=device-width, initial-scale=1.0">
    <title>My HTML5 Page</title>
    <link rel="stylesheet" href="css/styles.css">
    <script src="js/script.js" defer></script>
```

```html
</head>
<body>
  <header>
    <h1>Welcome to My HTML5 Page</h1>
  </header>

  <main>
    <section>
      <h2>About HTML5</h2>
      <p>HTML5 is a markup language used for structuring and presenting content on the web.</p>
    </section>

    <section>
      <h2>Features of HTML5</h2>
      <ul>
        <li>New semantic elements</li>
        <li>Support for audio and video</li>
        <li>Canvas element for graphics</li>
        <li>Improved form controls</li>
      </ul>
    </section>
  </main>
```

```
    <footer>
        <p>&copy; 2023 Your Name. All rights reserved.</p>
    </footer>
</body>
</html>
```

HTML5 Boilerplate

The HTML5 Boilerplate is a front-end template that helps you create fast, robust, and adaptable web applications or websites. It includes a minimalist development environment to ensure you start with the best practices in web development. Here's what's typically included in an HTML5 Boilerplate setup.

1. Boilerplate HTML Template

The essential elements of an HTML5 Boilerplate template look very similar to the complete document structure we discussed earlier with some enhancements.

```html
<!DOCTYPE html>
<html lang="en">
<head>
    <meta charset="UTF-8">
    <meta name="viewport" content="width=device-width, initial-scale=1.0">
    <title>Your Site Title - HTML5 Boilerplate</title>
    <link rel="stylesheet" href="css/styles.css">
    <script src="js/script.js" defer></script>
    <link rel="icon" href="images/favicon.ico">
</head>
<body>
    <header>
        <h1>Welcome to My Boilerplate Project</h1>
    </header>

    <main>
        <section>
            <h2>What is HTML5 Boilerplate?</h2>
            <p>HTML5 Boilerplate is a template
```

that provides you with a starting point for your web projects, ensuring that you have a solid foundation to work from.</p>
    </section>
  </main>

  <footer>
    <p>© 2023 Your Name. All rights reserved.</p>
  </footer>
</body>
</html>
```

### 2. CSS Files

The boilerplate may include a `styles.css` file with some default styles. For example:

```css
* {
  margin: 0;
  padding: 0;
  box-sizing: border-box;
}

body {

```css
    font-family: Arial, sans-serif;
    line-height: 1.6;
    background-color: #f4f4f4;
    color: #333;
}

header {
    background: #35424a;
    color: #ffffff;
    padding: 20px 0;
}

main {
    padding: 20px;
}
```

3. JavaScript Files

A `script.js` file can be included for your custom JavaScript functionality. For instance:

```javascript
document.addEventListener('DOMContentLoaded', function() {
    console.log("Document is fully loaded and parsed.");
```

});
```

### 4. Additional Resources

- You might also add links to popular libraries or frameworks within your HTML5 Boilerplate, such as:

```html
<link rel="stylesheet" href="https://cdnjs.cloudflare.com/ajax/libs/font-awesome/5.15.4/css/all.min.css">
<script src="https://code.jquery.com/jquery-3.6.0.min.js"></script>
```

5. SEO and Analytics

You can enhance your boilerplate with meta tags for SEO or scripts for web analytics. For example:

```html
<meta name="description" content="A brief description of the page.">
<meta name="robots" content="index,

```
follow">
<script async src="https://www.googletagmanager.com/gtag/js?id=YOUR_TRACKING_ID"></script>
<script>
   window.dataLayer = window.dataLayer || [];
   function gtag(){dataLayer.push(arguments);}
   gtag('js', new Date());
   gtag('config', 'YOUR_TRACKING_ID');
</script>
```

Conclusion

HTML5 is a powerful tool for building dynamic and interactive web applications. This guide has provided a roadmap for getting started with HTML5, setting up your development environment, understanding the basic structure of an HTML5 document, and creating a boilerplate to facilitate your web development projects.

As you start working with HTML5, remember to keep exploring its numerous features, such as multimedia support and new form elements, which can enhance your web development capabilities. With practice and experimentation, you will quickly become proficient in HTML5, paving the way for more complex projects and applications.

3. Understanding HTML5 Document Structure

HTML5 is the latest version of Hypertext Markup Language and represents a major leap in how web content is structured. An HTML5 document is structured in a particular way, which helps both browsers and developers understand and render web pages efficiently. The following sections break down the primary components of an HTML5 document structure and provide detailed explanations and examples of each.

The Doctype Declaration

The document type declaration, or "doctype," is the first line of an HTML document and instructs the web browser about the version of HTML the page is written in. For HTML5, the doctype is remarkably simple compared to previous versions.

Example:

```html
```

```
<!DOCTYPE html>
```

Explanation:

- **Purpose**: The doctype declaration is essential because it tells the browser to render the document in standards mode as per HTML5 specifications.
- **Format**: In HTML5, there is no need to specify the character set, so the declaration is straightforward. It is written in uppercase (`<!DOCTYPE html>`), but HTML is case-insensitive, so it can also be written in lowercase.

Importance:

1. **Standards Compliance**: Helps ensure that the page is rendered using the standards set forth by HTML5, promoting uniformity across different browsers.
2. **Legacy Support**: By declaring HTML5, you align yourself with modern web development practices, ensuring compatibility with newer technologies like CSS3 and JavaScript ES6.

The `<html>` Element

The `<html>` element is the root element of an HTML document and wraps all other elements, serving as a container for the entire webpage.

Example:

```html
<!DOCTYPE html>
<html lang="en">
</html>
```

Explanation:

- **Language Attribute**: The `lang` attribute specifies the primary language of the document's content, which improves accessibility and aids search engines and screen readers. In this example, it is set to English (`"en"`).
- **Usage**: The `<html>` element is followed by two main sections: `<head>` and `<body>`.

Importance:

1. **Semantic Structure**: It provides semantic meaning to the document, making the document more understandable.
2. **CSS Targeting**: The `<html>` element can also be targeted in CSS for global styles.

The `<head>` Element

The `<head>` element contains metadata (data about data) about the HTML document. It is not displayed directly on the web page but contains essential information that helps the browser handle the page.

Example:

```html
<head>
   <meta charset="UTF-8">
   <meta name="viewport" content="width=device-width, initial-scale=1.0">
   <title>My First HTML5 Document</title>
   <link rel="stylesheet" href="styles.css">
```

```
</head>
```

Explanation:

1. **Meta Tags**:
   - `<meta charset="UTF-8">`: Specifies the character encoding for the HTML document to support a wide range of characters.
   - `<meta name="viewport" content="width=device-width, initial-scale=1.0">`: Ensures that the page is responsive by setting the viewport width to the device width, especially for mobile users.

2. **Title**:
   - `<title>My First HTML5 Document</title>`: Sets the title of the webpage that appears on the browser's title bar or tab and is also utilized by search engines.

3. **Linking Stylesheets**:
   - `<link rel="stylesheet" href="styles.css">`: Links an external CSS file for styling the HTML document.

Importance:

1. **SEO and Usability**: The title and meta tags improve search engine optimization and usability.
2. **External Resources**: The `<head>` element is where you can connect scripts, stylesheets, and other resources, ensuring everything needed by the page is properly linked.

The `<body>` Element

The `<body>` element contains the actual content of the HTML document. This includes text, images, videos, and other media that users interact with.

Example:

```html
<body>
    <h1>Welcome to My First HTML5 Page!</h1>
    <p>This is a paragraph of text that describes the content of this page.</p>
    <img src="image.jpg" alt="A descriptive alt text">
```

```
    <a href="https://www.example.com">Visit Example.com</a>
</body>
```

Explanation:

1. **Content Elements**:
   - `<h1>`: This is a heading element, representing the most important heading on the page. Search engines consider `<h1>` significant for SEO.
   - `<p>`: A paragraph element. Text content is wrapped with `<p>` tags to define paragraphs.
   - `<img>`: An image element to include images. The `alt` attribute provides text for screen readers, contributing to accessibility.
   - `<a>`: An anchor tag used to create hyperlinks, allowing navigation to other resources.

2. **Structural Tags**: The `<body>` can include more structural tags such as `<div>`, `<section>`, `<article>`, etc., to further organize content.

Importance:

1. **User Interaction**: The `<body>` is where users interact with the content of your webpage.
2. **Layout Control**: Using CSS and structural elements within the `<body>`, developers can create complex layouts and ensure accessibility.

Complete Example of an HTML5 Document

To encapsulate all the parts we've explored, here's a complete example of a simple HTML5 document:

```html
<!DOCTYPE html>
<html lang="en">
<head>
   <meta charset="UTF-8">
   <meta name="viewport" content="width=device-width, initial-scale=1.0">
   <title>My First HTML5 Document</title>
   <link rel="stylesheet" href="styles.css">
```

```html
</head>
<body>
  <header>
    <h1>Welcome to My First HTML5 Page!</h1>
    <nav>
      <ul>
        <li><a href="#home">Home</a></li>
        <li><a href="#about">About</a></li>
        <li><a href="#contact">Contact</a></li>
      </ul>
    </nav>
  </header>

  <main>
    <section>
      <h2>About This Page</h2>
      <p>This is a paragraph of text that describes the content of this page. It provides some interesting facts and information!</p>
      <img src="image.jpg" alt="A descriptive alt text">
    </section>
```

```
        <section>
            <h2>Contact Information</h2>
            <p>If you have any questions, feel free to <a href="mailto:example@example.com">send me an email</a>.</p>
        </section>
    </main>

    <footer>
        <p>&copy; 2023 My First HTML5 Page. All rights reserved.</p>
    </footer>
</body>
</html>
```

Explanation of the Complete Example:

- **Header**: Contains the main title and navigation links within the `<header>` section.
- **Main Content**: Comprises multiple sections, describing the content relevant to the webpage. Each section is wrapped in a `<section>` tag, enhancing semantic meaning.
- **Footer**: Provides copyright information

and wraps the document with a `<footer>` element.

Conclusion

Understanding the structure of an HTML5 document is vital for any web developer or designer. This structure not only organizes the content for users but also enhances the way search engines interpret and rank the pages. By crafting a well-structured HTML5 document using the `<html>`, `<head>`, and `<body>` elements, developers can ensure optimal performance and user experience.

As web standards continue to evolve, familiarity with these foundational elements will enable developers to create dynamic, accessible, and aesthetically pleasing websites that adhere to modern web practices.

4. Overview of Semantic HTML

Semantic HTML is an essential aspect of modern web development that enhances both the meaning and accessibility of web content. Unlike non-semantic tags such as `<div>` and `<span>`, which define sections of a webpage without imparting any inherent meaning, semantic elements provide context and clarity about the content they encapsulate. This becomes particularly important for search engines, screen readers, and other technologies that parse web pages.

Semantic HTML has numerous advantages:

1. **Improved Accessibility**: Screen readers can interpret the content better, allowing visually impaired users to navigate web pages with greater ease.
2. **SEO Benefits**: Search engines can better understand the structure and content of your pages, which can improve rankings and visibility.
3. **Maintainability**: Semantic markup allows developers to create more intuitive and

organized code, making it easier to manage and update.
4. **Clearer Structure**: It allows developers and designers to communicate the purpose of elements on the page more clearly.

Let's explore various semantic HTML5 elements, elaborating on their purposes, usage, and how they contribute to a well-structured webpage.

Header Elements: `<header>`, `<nav>`, `<section>`, `<article>`, `<aside>`, `<footer>`

1. `<header>`

The `<header>` element represents the introductory content of a section or page. It typically contains headings, logos, and navigation links.

Example:

```html
<header>
    <h1>My Website Title</h1>
    <nav>
```

```
    <ul>
        <li><a href="#home">Home</a></li>
        <li><a href="#about">About</a></li>
        <li><a href="#services">Services</a></li>
        <li><a href="#contact">Contact</a></li>
    </ul>
  </nav>
</header>
```

2. `<nav>`

The `<nav>` element is used to define a set of navigation links. This can include menus, tables of contents, and any other navigational aids.

Example:

```html
<nav>
  <ul>
    <li><a href="#home">Home</a></li>
    <li><a href="#products">Products</a></li>
```

```
      <li><a href="#services">Services</a></li>
      <li><a href="#about">About</a></li>
   </ul>
</nav>
```

3. `<section>`

A `<section>` element is used to represent a thematic grouping of content, typically with a heading. Each section can stand alone, making it easy to understand the organization of the content.

Example:

```html
<section>
   <h2>About Us</h2>
   <p>Our company has been in business since 1990, providing excellent services to our clients.</p>
</section>
```

4. `<article>`

The `<article>` element is intended for self-contained content that could be distributed independently from the rest of the webpage. This is especially common for blog posts, news articles, or user comments.

Example:

```html
<article>
    <h2>Understanding Climate Change</h2>
    <p>Climate change is a significant and lasting change in the statistical distribution of weather patterns...</p>
    <footer>
        <p>Published on: April 10, 2021</p>
    </footer>
</article>
```

5. `<aside>`

The `<aside>` element represents content that is tangentially related to the content around it, often used for sidebars or additional information.

Example:

```html
<aside>
   <h3>Related Articles</h3>
   <ul>
     <li><a href="#climate-solutions">Solutions to Climate Change</a></li>
     <li><a href="#impact-on-economy">Impact on Economy</a></li>
   </ul>
</aside>
```

6. `<footer>`

The `<footer>` element is used for footer content, encapsulating information such as copyright notices, contact details, or links to related documents.

Example:

```html
<footer>
```

```
    <p>&copy; 2023 My Company. All rights reserved.</p>
    <ul>
        <li><a href="#privacy">Privacy Policy</a></li>
        <li><a href="#terms">Terms of Service</a></li>
    </ul>
</footer>
```

Usage of `<main>`, `<figure>`, and `<figcaption>`

1. `<main>`

The `<main>` element represents the dominant content of the `<body>` of a document. It is intended to contain unique content that is directly related to or expands upon the central topic.

Example:

```html
<main>
    <h1>Welcome to My Website</h1>
```

```
    <p>Here you will find a variety of articles,
tutorials, and resources.</p>

    <section>
        <h2>Latest Articles</h2>
        <article>
            <h3>Understanding HTML5 Semantic
Elements</h3>
            <p>HTML5 introduced several
semantic elements that help improve the
structure of web pages...</p>
        </article>
        <article>
            <h3>The Importance of
Accessibility</h3>
            <p>Accessibility is crucial for
ensuring that everyone can access and enjoy
web content...</p>
        </article>
    </section>
</main>
```

2. `<figure>`

The `<figure>` element is used to encapsulate media content like images, charts, or diagrams, along with their captions.

Example:

```html
<figure>
    <img src="climate_change.jpg" alt="Graph showing climate change trends">
    <figcaption>Graph illustrating the trends in global temperatures over the last century.</figcaption>
</figure>
```

3. `<figcaption>`

The `<figcaption>` element is used as a caption for the content inside a `<figure>`, providing an opportunity to explain or give context about the associated media.

Example:

```html
<figure>
    <img src="tech_conference.jpg" alt="Technology Conference 2023">
```

    <figcaption>Participants engaged in discussions at the Technology Conference 2023.</figcaption>
</figure>
```

## Conclusion

Semantic HTML5 elements play a vital role in creating meaningful and accessible web content. By using elements like `<header>`, `<nav>`, `<section>`, `<article>`, `<aside>`, `<footer>`, `<main>`, `<figure>`, and `<figcaption>`, developers can ensure that their web pages have a clear structure that is easily understood by both users and machines.

Incorporating semantic HTML not only improves usability and SEO but also enhances the overall user experience, making websites more engaging and informative. As web technologies continue to evolve, adhering to semantic guidelines will become increasingly important for developers aiming to create accessible, user-friendly digital environments. Thus, understanding and implementing these elements is critical for any modern web
```

developer or content creator.

5. Understanding Text and Inline Elements in HTML

HTML (HyperText Markup Language) is the standard markup language used to create web pages. One of the fundamental features of HTML is its ability to delineate text-based content using a variety of elements. This guide will explore text and inline elements extensively, focusing on headings, paragraphs, text formatting components, links, and lists. By the end of this document, you should have a thorough understanding of how to effectively use these elements in your web development projects.

Headings and Paragraphs

Headings and paragraphs are crucial for organizing content on web pages. HTML provides six levels of headings, ranging from `<h1>` to `<h6>`. Each level signifies a different level of importance, with `<h1>` being the highest.

Headings

Headings help structure the content and improve the accessibility of your text. Here's how they are typically used:

```html
<h1>This is a Level 1 Heading</h1>
<h2>This is a Level 2 Heading</h2>
<h3>This is a Level 3 Heading</h3>
<h4>This is a Level 4 Heading</h4>
<h5>This is a Level 5 Heading</h5>
<h6>This is a Level 6 Heading</h6>
```

Example Explanation:
- The `<h1>` element should be used for the main title of your page. It's usually reserved for the primary topic or purpose.
- Subsequent heading levels (`<h2>` to `<h6>`) help in organizing sub-sections of content, providing a clear hierarchy that makes it easier for users and search engines to understand the structure of your content.

Paragraphs

The `<p>` element represents a paragraph, which is used to group related sentences. Each paragraph will typically start on a new line and will automatically include some margin above and below to create spacing.

```html
<p>This is a paragraph of text that gives information about the topic introduced by the heading.
It contains multiple sentences and can be styled and formatted using CSS.</p>
```

Example Explanation:
- The example above demonstrates how content can be grouped into a paragraph, making it visually coherent and easy to read. You can also have multiple paragraphs on a page, each conveying different aspects of the topic.

Formatting Text: `<strong>`, `<em>`, `<del>`, `<mark>`, and More

HTML provides various inline elements, allowing you to emphasize or alter the appearance of text within paragraphs or other text blocks.

Bold and Italics

1. **`<strong>`**: This tag is used for strong importance and usually displays the text in bold.

```html
<p>This is a <strong>strong</strong> statement that needs highlighting.</p>
```

2. **`<em>`**: This tag emphasizes text and typically results in italicized text.

```html
<p>I really <em>enjoy</em> learning web development.</p>
```

Example Explanation:
- The `<strong>` tag is often used for text that carries higher significance, while `<em>` is used for adding emphasis, like highlighting a specific point or thought.

Deleted, Inserted, and Highlighted Text

In addition to bold and italics, you can also indicate text that has been removed or added and highlight important text:

1. **`<del>`**: Use this tag to show text that has been deleted.

```html
<p>The project deadline was <del>April 1st</del> <ins>May 1st</ins>.</p>
```

2. **`<ins>`**: This tag is for inserted text.

3. **`<mark>`**: Use this tag to highlight text, commonly seen when you want to draw attention to a specific part within your content.

```html
<p>Remember to <mark>highlight</mark> important information!</p>
```

Example Explanation:
- The example demonstrates how `<del>` and `<ins>` can effectively communicate changes, while `<mark>` is useful for user guidance or

denoting changes in emphasis.

Links: `<a>` Element

Links are an essential aspect of HTML, enabling navigation from one page to another or to different sections within the same page.

Using the `<a>` Element

The anchor tag `<a>` is the main element used for hyperlinks. Here's how it works:

```html
<a href="https://www.example.com">Visit Example.com</a>
```

Example Explanation:
- The `href` attribute specifies the URL where the link points. The text "Visit Example.com" will appear as a clickable link.

Internal Links

You can also link to different sections within the same page by using an ID:

```html
<h2 id="about">About Us</h2>
<p>This section provides information about our website.</p>

<a href="#about">Jump to About Us</a>
```

Example Explanation:
- By using `href="#about"`, clicking the link will take you to the "About Us" section of the same page.

Opening Links in a New Tab

You can open links in a new tab by using the `target` attribute:

```html
<a href="https://www.example.com" target="_blank">Visit Example.com in a new tab</a>
```

Lists: `<ul>`, `<ol>`, `<li>`

Lists are an effective way to present

information in an organized manner. HTML supports both ordered (numbered) and unordered (bulleted) lists.

Unordered Lists

An unordered list is defined by the `<ul>` tag. Each item is marked with the `<li>` tag.

```html
<ul>
  <li>Item 1</li>
  <li>Item 2</li>
  <li>Item 3</li>
</ul>
```

Example Explanation:
- This code creates a bulleted list where each item is presented with a bullet point.

Ordered Lists

Similar to unordered lists, an ordered list is defined using the `<ol>` tag:

```html
```

```html
<ol>
  <li>First Item</li>
  <li>Second Item</li>
  <li>Third Item</li>
</ol>
```

Example Explanation:
- This code results in a numbered list, perfect for presenting steps or ranked items.

Nested Lists

You can nest lists within each other for more complex arrangements:

```html
<ul>
  <li>Fruits
    <ul>
      <li>Apple</li>
      <li>Banana</li>
      <li>Cherry</li>
    </ul>
  </li>
  <li>Vegetables
    <ul>
```

```
      <li>Carrot</li>
      <li>Broccoli</li>
    </ul>
  </li>
</ul>
```

Example Explanation:
- This example demonstrates how to create hierarchical lists, grouping related items effectively.

By mastering these fundamental text and inline elements, you lay a strong foundation for your web development skills, allowing for better design, styling, and content management. Whether you're building a personal blog, a corporate website, or an online portfolio, these HTML elements will be indispensable in your toolkit.

6. Images and Multimedia in HTML5

HTML5 has revolutionized the way web developers handle multimedia content, providing robust and intuitive elements for embedding images, audio, video, and even graphics. This guide emphasizes key HTML5 elements, including `<img>`, `<video>`, `<audio>`, `<source>`, and `<canvas>`, elaborating on their uses, best practices, and examples.

The `<img>` Element

The `<img>` element is used to embed images in a web page. It is a self-closing tag that allows developers to display images directly on a webpage. The most commonly used attributes of the `<img>` element are:

- `src`: Specifies the path to the image file.
- `alt`: Provides alternative text for the image in case it cannot be displayed.
- `width`: Specifies the width of the image.
- `height`: Specifies the height of the image.
- `title`: Offers additional information about

the image, usually displayed as a tooltip when the user hovers over it.

Example:

Here is a basic example of using the `<img>` element:

```html
<!DOCTYPE html>
<html lang="en">
<head>
    <meta charset="UTF-8">
    <meta name="viewport" content="width=device-width, initial-scale=1.0">
    <title>Image Example</title>
</head>
<body>
    <h1>Welcome to My Image Gallery</h1>
    <img src="https://example.com/image.jpg" alt="A beautiful landscape" width="600" height="400" title="A breathtaking view of nature">
</body>
</html>
```

Responsive Images:

With the rise of responsive design, it's important to serve images that fit various screen sizes. The `<picture>` element can be used to provide multiple sources for different device resolutions and aspect ratios, along with the `<img>` element:

```html
<picture>
    <source media="(max-width: 600px)" srcset="small-image.jpg">
    <source media="(max-width: 1200px)" srcset="medium-image.jpg">
    <img src="large-image.jpg" alt="A beautiful landscape" style="width:auto;">
</picture>
```

This approach allows the browser to select the best image source based on current viewport size, thus improving page performance and user experience.

The `<video>` Element

The `<video>` element provides a straightforward way to embed video content directly into HTML documents. It supports several attributes:

- `src`: Specifies the URL of the video file.
- `controls`: A Boolean attribute that specifies whether video controls (play, pause, etc.) are displayed.
- `autoplay`: If present, the video will start playing automatically when it loads.
- `loop`: If present, the video will loop continuously.
- `muted`: If present, the video is muted by default.
- `poster`: A URL to an image that will be displayed while the video is downloading or until the user hits the play button.

Example:

Below is an example of how to embed a video using the `<video>` element:

```html
<!DOCTYPE html>
<html lang="en">
```

```html
<head>
    <meta charset="UTF-8">
    <meta name="viewport" content="width=device-width, initial-scale=1.0">
    <title>Video Example</title>
</head>
<body>
    <h1>My Favorite Video</h1>
    <video controls width="600" poster="thumbnail.jpg">
        <source src="video.mp4" type="video/mp4">
        <source src="video.ogg" type="video/ogg">
        Your browser does not support the video tag.
    </video>
</body>
</html>
```

Advanced Video Features:

HTML5 video elements can also be enhanced with JavaScript to create custom controls or even implement streaming capabilities. Here's an example where we create a play/pause button:

```html
<!DOCTYPE html>
<html lang="en">
<head>
    <meta charset="UTF-8">
    <meta name="viewport" content="width=device-width, initial-scale=1.0">
    <title>Video Controls Example</title>
    <style>
        button {
            margin-top: 10px;
        }
    </style>
</head>
<body>
    <h1>Custom Video Controls</h1>
    <video id="myVideo" width="600">
        <source src="video.mp4" type="video/mp4">
        Your browser does not support the video tag.
    </video>
    <button
```

```
onclick="togglePlay()">Play/Pause</button>

  <script>
    var video = document.getElementById("myVideo");
    function togglePlay() {
      if (video.paused) {
        video.play();
      } else {
        video.pause();
      }
    }
  </script>
</body>
</html>
```

The `<audio>` Element

Much like the `<video>` element, the `<audio>` element allows you to embed sound content in a webpage. Key attributes of the `<audio>` element include:

- `controls`: Displays audio controls in the browser.
- `autoplay`: If set, the audio will start playing

automatically.
- `loop`: If set, audio will loop continuously.
- `preload`: Defines how the audio should be loaded (e.g., "auto", "metadata", "none").

Example:

Here is a simple example of the `<audio>` element:

```html
<!DOCTYPE html>
<html lang="en">
<head>
   <meta charset="UTF-8">
   <meta name="viewport" content="width=device-width, initial-scale=1.0">
   <title>Audio Example</title>
</head>
<body>
   <h1>Listen to My Favorite Song</h1>
   <audio controls>
      <source src="audio.mp3" type="audio/mp3">
      <source src="audio.ogg" type="audio/ogg">
```

```
    Your browser does not support the audio element.
  </audio>
</body>
</html>
```

Implementing Advanced Audio Features:

You can also use JavaScript to create custom audio player interfaces. Here is an example:

```html
<!DOCTYPE html>
<html lang="en">
<head>
  <meta charset="UTF-8">
  <meta name="viewport" content="width=device-width, initial-scale=1.0">
  <title>Custom Audio Player</title>
  <style>
    button {
      margin-top: 10px;
    }
  </style>
</head>
```

```html
<body>
  <h1>Custom Audio Player</h1>
  <audio id="myAudio">
    <source src="audio.mp3" type="audio/mp3">
    Your browser does not support the audio element.
  </audio>
  <button onclick="togglePlay()">Play/Pause</button>

  <script>
    var audio = document.getElementById("myAudio");
    function togglePlay() {
      if (audio.paused) {
        audio.play();
      } else {
        audio.pause();
      }
    }
  </script>
</body>
</html>
```

The `<source>` Element

HTML5 provides the `<source>` element as a way to specify multiple media resources (for both images and audio/video) for the same media element. The browser will select the first compatible source.

Use in Video:

```html
<video controls>
   <source src="video.mp4" type="video/mp4">
   <source src="video.webm" type="video/webm">
   Your browser does not support the video tag.
</video>
```

Use in Audio:

```html
<audio controls>
   <source src="audio.mp3" type="audio/mp3">
   <source src="audio.ogg" type="audio/ogg">
```

    Your browser does not support the audio element.
    </audio>
```

### Best Practices with `<source>`:

- Always provide multiple formats of audio and video files to cater to varying browser support.
- Utilize file types like Ogg and WebM for compatibility with browsers that do not support MP4 due to licensing issues.
- Leverage the `type` attribute in each `<source>` element to specify the MIME type.

## Using `<canvas>` for Graphics

The `<canvas>` element provides a space on the web page to draw graphics via scripting (JavaScript). This can be used for graphics, animations, games, and more. It is a versatile element that allows for dynamic rendering.

### Attributes of `<canvas>`:

- `width`: Specifies the width of the canvas.
```

- `height`: Specifies the height of the canvas.

Basic Drawing Example:

Here's a simple example of using the `<canvas>` element:

```html
<!DOCTYPE html>
<html lang="en">
<head>
    <meta charset="UTF-8">
    <meta name="viewport" content="width=device-width, initial-scale=1.0">
    <title>Canvas Example</title>
</head>
<body>
    <h1>My Canvas Drawing</h1>
    <canvas id="myCanvas" width="300" height="200" style="border:1px solid #000000;"></canvas>
    <script>
        var canvas = document.getElementById("myCanvas");
        var ctx = canvas.getContext("2d");
```

```
    // Draw a rectangle
    ctx.fillStyle = "#FF0000";
    ctx.fillRect(20, 20, 150, 100);
  </script>
</body>
</html>
```

Advanced Graphics with Canvas:

You can create more complex drawings by utilizing methods like `arc()` for circles, `beginPath()` for paths, and gradients for colors. Here's how you can integrate these concepts:

```html
<!DOCTYPE html>
<html lang="en">
<head>
   <meta charset="UTF-8">
   <meta name="viewport" content="width=device-width, initial-scale=1.0">
   <title>Advanced Canvas Drawing</title>
</head>
<body>
```

```html
<h1>Canvas Graphics Example</h1>
<canvas id="myCanvas" width="500" height="400" style="border:1px solid #000;"></canvas>
<script>
    var canvas = document.getElementById("myCanvas");
    var ctx = canvas.getContext("2d");

    // Draw a circle
    ctx.beginPath();
    ctx.arc(240, 200, 100, 0, Math.PI * 2, true); // Outer circle
    ctx.fillStyle = "blue";
    ctx.fill();
    ctx.closePath();

    // Draw a triangle
    ctx.beginPath();
    ctx.moveTo(350, 100);
    ctx.lineTo(400, 200);
    ctx.lineTo(300, 200);
    ctx.fillStyle = "green";
    ctx.fill();
    ctx.closePath();
</script>
</body>
```

```
</html>
```

Canvas Animations:

You can create animations with the `<canvas>` element using the `requestAnimationFrame` function, allowing for smooth transitions:

```html
<!DOCTYPE html>
<html lang="en">
<head>
    <meta charset="UTF-8">
    <meta name="viewport" content="width=device-width, initial-scale=1.0">
    <title>Canvas Animation</title>
</head>
<body>
    <h1>Bouncing Ball Animation</h1>
    <canvas id="myCanvas" width="500" height="400" style="border:1px solid #000;"></canvas>
    <script>
        var canvas =
```

```javascript
document.getElementById("myCanvas");
    var ctx = canvas.getContext("2d");

    var x = canvas.width / 2;
    var y = canvas.height / 2;
    var dx = 2;
    var dy = -2;
    var ballRadius = 10;

    function drawBall() {
       ctx.beginPath();
       ctx.arc(x, y, ballRadius, 0, Math.PI * 2);
       ctx.fillStyle = "#0095DD";
       ctx.fill();
       ctx.closePath();
    }

    function draw() {
       ctx.clearRect(0, 0, canvas.width, canvas.height);
       drawBall();
       x += dx;
       y += dy;
       if (x + dx > canvas.width - ballRadius || x + dx < ballRadius) {
          dx = -dx;
```

```
        }
        if (y + dy > canvas.height - ballRadius || y + dy < ballRadius) {
            dy = -dy;
        }
        requestAnimationFrame(draw);
    }

    draw();
  </script>
</body>
</html>
```

This guide serves as a foundation for you to explore and implement these elements effectively in your web projects. As you continue developing, keep practicing the provided examples and concepts, and consider exploring additional features and attributes available in HTML5 for a richer multimedia experience.

7. Forms in HTML5

HTML forms are essential components of web applications that enable users to submit data to web servers. With the advent of HTML5, forms have evolved, making it easier to create and handle user input efficiently. HTML5 introduces new input types, attributes, and elements that enhance user experience, improve accessibility, and enable developers to validate input with fewer scripts. This document outlines an overview of HTML forms, the new input types in HTML5, essential form attributes, the purpose of the `<datalist>` element, and considerations for accessibility in forms.

Overview of HTML Forms

HTML forms are represented within the `<form>` element and contain various types of input fields. These fields allow users to enter data that is usually sent to a server for processing. The basic structure of an HTML form includes:

- Input fields for user data (text, checkboxes, radio buttons, etc.)
- Labels that describe each input field
- Buttons for submission and resetting the form

Here's a simple example of an HTML form:

```html
<form action="/submit" method="POST">
    <label for="username">Username:</label>
    <input type="text" id="username" name="username" required>

    <label for="password">Password:</label>
    <input type="password" id="password" name="password" required>

    <input type="submit" value="Submit">
    <input type="reset" value="Reset">
</form>
```

Key Components

1. **Action Attribute**: The URL where the form data will be submitted.

2. **Method Attribute**: Specifies how to send form data (`GET` or `POST`).
3. **Input Elements**: Various fields for user inputs.
4. **Labels**: Assistive text associated with corresponding input fields ensuring better clarity.

New Input Types: Date, Email, Number, Range, etc.

HTML5 introduces new input types designed to improve user experience. These input types enhance data validation and provide appropriate user interfaces.

New Input Types

1. **Date**: Provides a date picker in supported browsers.

```html
<label for="birthdate">Birthdate:</label>
<input type="date" id="birthdate" name="birthdate" required>
```

2. **Email**: Ensures the user inputs a valid email format, provides a keyboard optimized for email entry on mobile devices.

```html
<label for="email">Email:</label>
<input type="email" id="email" name="email" required>
```

3. **Number**: Facilitates numeric input with up/down controls.

```html
<label for="quantity">Quantity:</label>
<input type="number" id="quantity" name="quantity" min="1" max="100" required>
```

4. **Range**: Allows the selection of a numeric value from a range using a slider.

```html
<label for="volumes">Volume:</label>
<input type="range" id="volumes" name="volumes" min="0" max="100"
```

step="10">
```

5. **Tel**: Designed for entering phone numbers.

```html
<label for="telephone">Telephone:</label>
<input type="tel" id="telephone" name="telephone">
```

6. **Url**: Validates that the user inputs a valid URL format.

```html
<label for="website">Website:</label>
<input type="url" id="website" name="website">
```

These input types not only validate user input but also enhance mobile usability by presenting the appropriate keyboard.

Form Attributes: Placeholder, Required, Pattern
```

HTML5 provides several attributes that further improve form usability and validation.

Common Form Attributes

1. **Placeholder**: Displays a short hint within the input field, guiding users on what to enter.

```html
<label for="username">Username:</label>
<input type="text" id="username" name="username" placeholder="Enter your username" required>
```

2. **Required**: Specifies that an input field must be filled out before submitting the form.

```html
<label for="email">Email:</label>
<input type="email" id="email" name="email" required>
```

3. **Pattern**: Uses a regular expression to

validate the input value. This attribute is particularly useful for ensuring more complex input formats.

```html
<label for="postalcode">Postal Code:</label>
<input type="text" id="postalcode" name="postalcode" pattern="[0-9]{5}" placeholder="e.g. 12345" required>
```

These attributes significantly reduce the need for JavaScript validation, providing built-in mechanisms for basic error checking.

The `<datalist>` Element

The `<datalist>` element provides a predefined list of options for an `<input>` element. Users can either select from the list or input their values, enhancing user experience and reducing input errors.

```html
<label for="car">Choose a car:</label>
<input list="cars" id="car" name="car">
<datalist id="cars">
```

```
    <option value="Volvo">
    <option value="Saab">
    <option value="Mercedes">
    <option value="Audi">
</datalist>
```

Benefits of Using `<datalist>`

- **Flexible Input**: Users can select from a list but are not limited to those options; they can also enter their choices.
- **Improved Usability**: List options can speed up data entry and reduce errors.
- **Cross-browser Compatibility**: Most modern browsers support `<datalist>`, making it a reliable option for developers.

Accessibility Considerations for Forms

When designing forms, accessibility should be a foremost concern, ensuring that all users, including those with disabilities, can use them effectively. Here are key considerations for enhancing form accessibility:

Best Practices for Accessible Forms

1. **Use Labels**: Always associate labels with their corresponding input fields using the `for` attribute. This is crucial for screen readers.

```html
<label for="username">Username:</label>
<input type="text" id="username" name="username">
```

2. **Tab Order**: Ensure a logical tab order in forms, allowing users to navigate through form fields easily using the keyboard.

3. **Error Identification**: Clearly identify errors in form submission. Users should receive specific feedback about what needs to be corrected.

```html
<p style="color:red;" id="error">Please enter a valid email address.</p>
```

4. **Keyboard Accessibility**: Ensure that all interactive elements can be accessed and

activated through the keyboard.

5. **Use ARIA Roles if Necessary**: If forms become complex, ARIA (Accessible Rich Internet Applications) roles can be used to enhance screen reader accessibility.

6. **Visual Contrast**: Ensure that text elements (labels, error messages, etc.) have sufficient contrast with the background to be easily readable.

Testing Accessibility

To ensure forms are accessible, developers can use tools such as:

- **Screen Readers**: Tools like NVDA (NonVisual Desktop Access) or VoiceOver (on macOS) allow developers to check how forms are read by assistive technology.
- **Automated Accessibility Checkers**: Tools like aXe, WAVE, or Lighthouse can identify common accessibility issues within web pages.

Understanding and utilizing these features in HTML5 forms can dramatically improve both the usability and accessibility of web applications, paving the way for a more inclusive web environment. By continuously exploring and implementing these advancements, developers can create robust and user-friendly web forms.

8. Introduction to HTML5 APIs

HTML5 introduced a plethora of new features and APIs (Application Programming Interfaces) that have transformed web development. These APIs enable developers to build more powerful, interactive, and dynamic web applications. Whereas HTML was primarily about structure, HTML5 embraces APIs that enhance functionality, allowing developers to create rich user experiences without relying on third-party plugins. This guide will detail some of the most important HTML5 APIs: the Geolocation API, Drag and Drop API, Web Storage API (Local Storage and Session Storage), Web Workers, and the Canvas API.

Geolocation API

The Geolocation API allows web applications to obtain the geographical location of a user. This can be particularly useful for applications that involve location-based services, such as mapping services, location tracking, or any application that provides content based on a user's geographical position.

Example Usage of the Geolocation API

Here's a simple example of how to use the Geolocation API to get a user's current position:

```html
<!DOCTYPE html>
<html lang="en">
<head>
    <meta charset="UTF-8">
    <meta name="viewport" content="width=device-width, initial-scale=1.0">
    <title>Geolocation Example</title>
</head>
<body>

<h1>Get Your Location</h1>
<button onclick="getLocation()">Find My Location</button>
<p id="location"></p>

<script>
    function getLocation() {
```

```javascript
    if (navigator.geolocation) {

navigator.geolocation.getCurrentPosition(showPosition, showError);
    } else {

document.getElementById("location").innerHTML = "Geolocation is not supported by this browser.";
    }
  }

  function showPosition(position) {
    const lat = position.coords.latitude;
    const long = position.coords.longitude;

document.getElementById("location").innerHTML = "Latitude: " + lat +
    "<br>Longitude: " + long;
  }

  function showError(error) {
    switch(error.code) {
      case error.PERMISSION_DENIED:

document.getElementById("location").innerHTML = "User denied the request for
```

```
Geolocation."
            break;
        case error.POSITION_UNAVAILABLE:
            document.getElementById("location").innerHTML = "Location information is unavailable."
            break;
        case error.TIMEOUT:
            document.getElementById("location").innerHTML = "The request to get user location timed out."
            break;
        case error.UNKNOWN_ERROR:
            document.getElementById("location").innerHTML = "An unknown error occurred."
            break;
    }
}
</script>

</body>
</html>
```

Explanation

In this example, we define a button that calls the `getLocation()` function when clicked. If the user allows the application to access their location, the `getCurrentPosition` method retrieves their coordinates. We display the coordinates on the web page. Error handling is also implemented to provide feedback if something goes wrong, such as if the user denies permission to access their location.

Drag and Drop API

The Drag and Drop API makes it easier to implement drag-and-drop functionality in web applications. It allows users to drag items around and drop them in designated areas, making for a more interactive user experience. This can be especially useful for applications like file uploads, image galleries, and sortable lists.

Example Usage of the Drag and Drop API

Here's a basic example of a drag-and-drop interface:

```html
<!DOCTYPE html>
<html lang="en">
<head>
  <meta charset="UTF-8">
  <meta name="viewport" content="width=device-width, initial-scale=1.0">
  <title>Drag and Drop Example</title>
  <style>
    #drag1 {
      width: 100px;
      height: 100px;
      background-color: yellow;
      margin: 10px;
      padding: 10px;
      border: 1px solid #ccc;
      display: inline-block;
      cursor: move;
    }

    #div2 {
      width: 200px;
      height: 200px;
      border: 1px solid #000;
      margin-top: 10px;
    }
```

```html
    </style>
  </head>
  <body>

  <h2>Drag and Drop Example</h2>
  <div id="drag1" draggable="true"
  ondragstart="drag(event)">Drag me!</div>
  <div id="div2" ondrop="drop(event)"
  ondragover="allowDrop(event)"></div>

  <script>
    function allowDrop(ev) {
      ev.preventDefault();
    }

    function drag(ev) {
      ev.dataTransfer.setData("text", ev.target.id);
    }

    function drop(ev) {
      ev.preventDefault();
      var data = ev.dataTransfer.getData("text");
      ev.target.appendChild(document.getElementById(data));
```

```
    }
</script>

</body>
</html>
```

Explanation

In this example, a yellow box can be dragged and dropped into a designated drop zone (the `div2` element). The `draggable` attribute is set to true, enabling dragging. The `ondragstart` event triggers the `drag()` function, which captures the ID of the dragged element. The `ondrop` event triggers the `drop()` function, which appends the dragged item to the drop zone. The `ondragover` event calls the `allowDrop()` function to prevent the default handling of the element, allowing it to accept drops.

Web Storage API: Local Storage and Session Storage

HTML5 introduced the Web Storage API, which provides a more robust and flexible solution for storing data in the web browser. The Web Storage API consists of two mechanisms: Local Storage and Session Storage.

- **Local Storage** is used to store data with no expiration date. The data persists even after the browser is closed and reopened.
- **Session Storage** is used to store data for a single session, meaning the data is cleared when the page session ends.

Example Usage of Web Storage API

Here's a simple example that demonstrates both Local Storage and Session Storage.

```html
<!DOCTYPE html>
<html lang="en">
<head>
    <meta charset="UTF-8">
    <meta name="viewport" content="width=device-width, initial-scale=1.0">
    <title>Web Storage Example</title>
</head>
```

```html
<body>

<h1>Web Storage Example</h1>
<input type="text" id="localInput" placeholder="Local Storage Input">
<button onclick="saveToLocal()">Save to Local Storage</button>
<button onclick="loadFromLocal()">Load from Local Storage</button>
<p id="localOutput"></p>

<input type="text" id="sessionInput" placeholder="Session Storage Input">
<button onclick="saveToSession()">Save to Session Storage</button>
<button onclick="loadFromSession()">Load from Session Storage</button>
<p id="sessionOutput"></p>

<script>
    function saveToLocal() {
        const input = document.getElementById('localInput').value;
        localStorage.setItem('localData', input);
    }

    function loadFromLocal() {
```

```
      const data = localStorage.getItem('localData');

document.getElementById('localOutput').innerText = data ? data : 'No data in Local Storage';
    }

  function saveToSession() {
      const input = document.getElementById('sessionInput').value;
      sessionStorage.setItem('sessionData', input);
    }

  function loadFromSession() {
      const data = sessionStorage.getItem('sessionData');

document.getElementById('sessionOutput').innerText = data ? data : 'No data in Session Storage';
    }
</script>

</body>
```

```
</html>
```

Explanation

This example features two separate inputs and buttons for handling both Local Storage and Session Storage. When the user enters data into the respective input fields and clicks the save buttons, the data is stored accordingly. If the user then clicks the load buttons, the stored data will be retrieved and displayed. Local Storage retains information even if the browser is closed, while Session Storage will be cleared once the tab or window is closed.

Web Workers

Web Workers provide a way to run JavaScript scripts in background threads, separate from the main thread that is responsible for rendering the web page. This allows for concurrent execution of code, making it possible to perform intensive computations without blocking the user interface.

Example Usage of Web Workers

To implement a simple Web Worker, create a new JavaScript file (e.g., `worker.js`) that the worker will execute:

worker.js
```javascript
self.onmessage = function(e) {
   let count = 0;
   for (let i = 0; i < e.data; i++) {
      count++;
   }
   self.postMessage(count);
};
```

index.html
```html
<!DOCTYPE html>
<html lang="en">
<head>
   <meta charset="UTF-8">
   <meta name="viewport" content="width=device-width, initial-scale=1.0">
   <title>Web Worker Example</title>
</head>
<body>
```

```html
<h1>Web Worker Example</h1>
<button onclick="startWorker()">Start Worker</button>
<p id="result"></p>

<script>
  let worker;

  function startWorker() {
    if (typeof(Worker) !== "undefined") {
      if (worker) {
        worker.terminate();
      }
      worker = new Worker("worker.js");
      worker.onmessage = function(event) {
        document.getElementById("result").innerText = "Count is: " + event.data;
      };
      worker.postMessage(1000000000); // Start counting
    } else {
      document.getElementById("result").innerText = "Sorry, your browser does not support web workers.";
    }
```

```
    }
  </script>

</body>
</html>
```

Explanation

In this example, we start a web worker when the user clicks the button. The worker executes the code in `worker.js`, which counts up to a number sent by the main thread. Once the worker completes its task, it sends the result back. Since the worker runs in the background, the user interface remains responsive.

Canvas API

The Canvas API provides a means to draw graphics on the web. It enables developers to create dynamic graphics, animations, and other visual representations programmatically within the browser. This API has broad applications, including game development, visual data representation, and image manipulation.

Example Usage of Canvas API

Here's a basic example of how to use the Canvas API:

```html
<!DOCTYPE html>
<html lang="en">
<head>
    <meta charset="UTF-8">
    <meta name="viewport" content="width=device-width, initial-scale=1.0">
    <title>Canvas API Example</title>
</head>
<body>

<h1>Canvas API Example</h1>
<canvas id="myCanvas" width="400" height="400" style="border:1px solid #000000;"></canvas>
<button onclick="draw()">Draw</button>

<script>
    function draw() {
```

```
      const canvas = document.getElementById("myCanvas");
      const ctx = canvas.getContext("2d");

      // Draw a rectangle
      ctx.fillStyle = "#FF0000";
      ctx.fillRect(20, 20, 150, 100);

      // Draw a circle
      ctx.beginPath();
      ctx.arc(240, 70, 50, 0, 2 * Math.PI);
      ctx.fillStyle = "blue";
      ctx.fill();

      // Draw a line
      ctx.beginPath();
      ctx.moveTo(250, 150);
      ctx.lineTo(350, 150);
      ctx.strokeStyle = "green";
      ctx.stroke();
    }
</script>

</body>
</html>
```

Explanation

In this example, we set up a canvas and a button. When the button is clicked, the `draw()` function is triggered. Inside this function, we first get the 2D rendering context from the canvas and then draw a filled rectangle, a filled circle, and a line. The Canvas API allows for a wide range of drawing operations, making it a powerful tool for creating graphics programmatically.

HTML5 introduces numerous APIs that significantly enhance web application capabilities. The Geolocation API allows for location tracking, the Drag and Drop API facilitates interactive interfaces, the Web Storage API provides a storage solution, Web Workers enable background processing, and the Canvas API allows for dynamic graphic drawing.

By understanding and utilizing these APIs, developers can create sophisticated and responsive web applications that greatly improve user experiences. As you dive deeper into each of these APIs, you'll find countless possibilities to integrate them into your projects, enhancing functionality, performance, and interactivity. Embrace the power of HTML5 APIs, and explore the exciting world of modern web development!

9. Responsive Web Design in HTML5

What is Responsive Design?

Responsive Web Design (RWD) is an approach to web development aimed at allowing web applications and websites to render well on a variety of devices and screen sizes. This includes everything from desktops and laptops to tablets and mobile phones. The core idea behind responsive design is to ensure that the user experience is optimal, regardless of the device being used to access the website.

Responsive design incorporates fluid grids, flexible images, and CSS media queries. The goal is to create a seamless experience that adapts to the user's environment, ensuring that they can access the content easily without excessive scrolling or zooming.

Benefits of Responsive Design

1. **Improved User Experience**: RWD enhances usability by providing an interface that adapts to different devices. This means

that users don't need to pinch and zoom to navigate; they can easily read and interact with the content.

2. **Cost-effective**: A single responsive site translates into lower development and maintenance costs compared to separate mobile sites.

3. **SEO Benefits**: Search engines, particularly Google, favor responsive sites. This is because a single responsive URL makes it easier for search engines to crawl, index, and organize content.

4. **Future-proofing**: Responsive design ensures that websites look good on all devices, which means they can accommodate future devices and resolutions.

Viewport Meta Tag

The viewport meta tag is a crucial component of responsive design. It allows the browser to control the dimensions and scaling of the webpage. Without this tag, web pages may not display correctly on smaller screens. The viewport tag needs to be included within the `<head>` section of your HTML document.

Example of Viewport Meta Tag

```html
<!DOCTYPE html>
<html lang="en">
<head>
    <meta charset="UTF-8">
    <meta name="viewport" content="width=device-width, initial-scale=1.0">
    <title>Responsive Design Example</title>
</head>
<body>
    <h1>Welcome to My Responsive Page</h1>
    <p>This is an example of a responsive web page using HTML5.</p>
</body>
</html>
```

In the example above, the viewport tag specifies that the width of the viewport should be equal to the width of the device, and the initial scale of the page is set to 1. This ensures that page elements render correctly on both small and large screens.

CSS Media Queries

CSS media queries are a fundamental technique used in responsive design to apply different styles depending on the device's characteristics, mainly its width. Media queries allow developers to create a design that responds to specific conditions.

Basic Syntax of Media Queries

The general syntax of a media query is as follows:

```css
@media media-type and (condition) {
    /* CSS rules here */
}
```

Example of CSS Media Queries

Here's an example demonstrating how you

can change the background color and font size based on different screen widths.

```html
<!DOCTYPE html>
<html lang="en">
<head>
  <meta charset="UTF-8">
  <meta name="viewport" content="width=device-width, initial-scale=1.0">
  <title>CSS Media Queries Example</title>
  <style>
    body {
      font-family: Arial, sans-serif;
      margin: 0;
      padding: 0;
      background-color: lightblue;
    }

    @media (max-width: 600px) {
      body {
        background-color: lightcoral;
        font-size: 14px;
      }
    }
```

```
    @media (min-width: 601px) and (max-width: 1200px) {
      body {
        background-color: lightgreen;
        font-size: 18px;
      }
    }

    @media (min-width: 1201px) {
      body {
        background-color: lightblue;
        font-size: 22px;
      }
    }
  </style>
</head>
<body>
  <h1>Responsive Design using CSS Media Queries</h1>
  <p>Resize the browser window to see the background color and font size change!</p>
</body>
</html>
```

In the above code:
- When the screen width is 600px or less, the

background color changes to light coral and the font size to 14px.
- When the width is between 601px and 1200px, the background color changes to light green and the font size increases to 18px.
- For screens wider than 1200px, the page switches back to light blue with a larger font size of 22px.

Creating Flexible Layouts

Flexible layouts utilize percentages rather than fixed values for widths, ensuring that elements adjust based on the viewport size. Grid systems and flexible box layouts are common methods to achieve this.

Example of a Flexible Layout Using CSS Flexbox

Flexbox is a modern layout model that allows you to design complex layouts more easily. Below is an example of a responsive layout using Flexbox to create a simple two-column design that stacks on smaller screens.

```html
```

```html
<!DOCTYPE html>
<html lang="en">
<head>
  <meta charset="UTF-8">
  <meta name="viewport" content="width=device-width, initial-scale=1.0">
  <title>Flexible Layout Example</title>
  <style>
    body {
      font-family: Arial, sans-serif;
      margin: 0;
      padding: 20px;
    }

    .container {
      display: flex;
      flex-wrap: wrap;
    }

    .column {
      flex: 50%; /* Two columns */
      padding: 10px;
    }

    @media (max-width: 600px) {
      .column {
```

```css
        flex: 100%; /* Stack on smaller screens */
    }
  }

    .box {
        background-color: lightblue;
        border: 1px solid #ccc;
        padding: 20px;
        box-shadow: 0 0 10px rgba(0, 0, 0, 0.1);
        min-height: 100px; /* Minimum height for demonstration */
    }
  </style>
</head>
<body>
  <h1>Responsive Flexible Layout with Flexbox</h1>
  <div class="container">
    <div class="column"><div class="box">Column 1 Content</div></div>
    <div class="column"><div class="box">Column 2 Content</div></div>
  </div>
</body>
</html>
```

```

In this layout:
- Two columns share equal space in a flex container.
- When the screen width is less than or equal to 600px, the columns stack vertically, making better use of the screen real estate on smaller devices.

### Creating a Responsive Image

Images often pose a challenge in responsive web design. To make an image responsive, set its `max-width` to 100% and its height to `auto`. This allows images to scale down with their parent container while maintaining their aspect ratio.

#### Example of Responsive Images

```html
<!DOCTYPE html>
<html lang="en">
<head>
    <meta charset="UTF-8">
    <meta name="viewport"

```
content="width=device-width, initial-scale=1.0">
  <title>Responsive Images Example</title>
  <style>
    .responsive-image {
      max-width: 100%;
      height: auto;
    }
  </style>
</head>
<body>
  <h1>Responsive Image Example</h1>
  <img src="example-image.jpg" alt="Example" class="responsive-image">
</body>
</html>
```

In this example, regardless of the screen size, the image will scale responsively, thereby enhancing the overall design and layout.

Responsive Web Design is an essential technique in modern web development. By utilizing the viewport meta tag, CSS media queries, and flexible layouts, you can create websites that seamlessly adapt to a variety of devices, ensuring an optimal user experience. With the rising number of devices accessing the web, responsive design is no longer just an option; it is a necessity for any web application aiming to reach a diverse audience.

Continual testing and refinement are also necessary to keep your website responsive across all platforms. Responsive design, when executed properly, not only enhances usability but can also improve your site's SEO standing, making it a vital skill for any web developer today. With the tools and techniques described, you will be well-equipped to build and maintain responsive websites that cater to all users.

10. Accessibility in HTML5

Introduction to Web Accessibility

Web accessibility refers to the design and development of websites, applications, and services that are usable by people with disabilities. This includes people who may have visual, auditory, motor, or cognitive limitations. According to the World Health Organization, about 15% of the global population experiences some form of disability, making it imperative that we create online experiences that everyone can engage with.

Importance of Web Accessibility

1. **Legal Obligations:** Many countries have laws requiring digital accessibility. For instance, in the U.S., the Americans with Disabilities Act (ADA) has been interpreted to apply to websites. Non-compliance can result in lawsuits or penalties.

2. **Market Reach:** By making your website accessible, you extend your reach to a

significant demographic. This includes individuals with disabilities and aging populations, who may face difficulties navigating typical web interfaces.

3. **Improved User Experience:** Accessibility features often lead to better usability for all users. Features intended for users with disabilities can improve the overall experience for everyone, from better navigation to more intuitive interfaces.

4. **SEO Benefits:** Search engines appreciate accessible websites. Elements like alternative text descriptions and semantic HTML can boost your visibility in search engine results.

Accessibility Standards

Several guidelines and standards govern web accessibility:

- **Web Content Accessibility Guidelines (WCAG):** A set of guidelines published by the World Wide Web Consortium (W3C) that outlines how to make web content more accessible to people with disabilities.

- **Section 508:** A part of the Rehabilitation Act in the U.S., which requires federal agencies to make their electronic and information technology accessible to people with disabilities.

These guidelines provide specific criteria to measure accessibility, categorized into levels (A, AA, AAA) based on compliance.

ARIA Roles and Properties

The Accessible Rich Internet Applications (ARIA) specification is a critical tool for enhancing web accessibility. ARIA defines ways to make web content and applications more accessible to people with disabilities, particularly those who rely on assistive technologies like screen readers.

ARIA Roles

Roles help define what an element is or does. Here are some common ARIA roles:

1. **`role="navigation"`:** Indicates a set of navigation links.
   ```html
   <nav role="navigation">
     <ul>
         <li><a href="#home">Home</a></li>
         <li><a href="#about">About Us</a></li>
         <li><a href="#services">Services</a></li>
     </ul>
   </nav>
   ```

2. **`role="banner"`:** Represents the header of a site, typically containing the logo and introductory content.
   ```html
   <header role="banner">
      <h1>Welcome to Our Website</h1>
   </header>
   ```

3. **`role="main"`:** Defines the main content of the document.
   ```html
   <main role="main">
   ```

```
    <h2>Main Content Area</h2>
    <p>This is where the main content will be displayed.</p>
   </main>
```

4. **`role="complementary"`:** Used for content that, while related to the surrounding content, is not essential to understanding it.
   ```html
   <aside role="complementary">
     <h2>Related Information</h2>
     <p>Additional context can be provided here.</p>
   </aside>
   ```

ARIA Properties and States

ARIA properties and states further enhance accessibility by providing additional context about elements. Here are some examples:

1. **`aria-label`:** Provides an accessible label for an element.
   ```html
   <button aria-label="Close"
   ```

```
onclick="closeModal()">
    <span aria-hidden="true">&times;</span>
  </button>
```

2. **`aria-labelledby`:** Associates an element with another element that provides its label.
```html
<h1 id="heading">Profile</h1>
<div role="dialog" aria-labelledby="heading">
    <p>This is the profile information.</p>
</div>
```

3. **`aria-hidden`:** Indicates that an element is not visible and should not be exposed to accessibility APIs.
```html
<div aria-hidden="true">
    This content is visually hidden and will not be announced.
</div>
```

4. **`aria-expanded`:** Indicates whether a section of the interface that can be expanded or collapsed is currently expanded or not.
```html
<button aria-expanded="false" onclick="toggleMenu()">Menu</button>
```

Best Practices for Accessible HTML

Creating accessible HTML involves following certain best practices to ensure compliance with accessibility standards. Here are some fundamental guidelines:

1. **Use Semantic HTML:** Use HTML markup according to its intended purpose. For instance, use `<header>`, `<footer>`, `<article>`, `<nav>`, and `<main>` instead of generic `<div>` elements. This helps assistive technologies interpret the document structure properly.

   Example:
```html
<article>
    <h2>A Brief History of Web
```

Development</h2>
    <p>The web has evolved significantly...</p>
  </article>
```

2. **Provide Text Alternatives:** Ensure that all non-text content, such as images, videos, and audio, have equivalent textual alternatives. Use the `alt` attribute for images to describe their function.

   Example:
   ```html
   <img src="logo.png" alt="Company Logo">
   ```

3. **Ensure Sufficient Color Contrast:** Text color should contrast sufficiently with its background to be readable by users with visual impairments. Use tools or contrast checkers to verify adequate color contrast.

4. **Use Correct Heading Levels:** Use headings (`<h1>` to `<h6>`) in a logical manner to structure content. This aids screen reader users in navigating the document
   ```

layout.

Example:
```html
<h1>Main Title</h1>
<h2>Section Title</h2>
<h3>Subsection Title</h3>
```

5. **Label Form Elements:** All forms and controls should be properly labeled. Use the `<label>` element to provide clear descriptions for form inputs.

Example:
```html
<label for="email">Email Address:</label>
<input type="email" id="email" name="email" required>
```

6. **Keyboard Navigation:** Ensure that all interactive elements can be accessed via keyboard navigation alone. This benefits users with mobility impairments and those who prefer keyboard usage over a mouse.

7. **Meaningful Link Text:** Use descriptive text for hyperlinks rather than generic terms like "click here" or "read more." This helps all users understand where the link will take them.

   Example:
   ```html
   <a href="https://www.example.com/services">Explore Our Services</a>
   ```

8. **Avoid Automatic Content Changes:** Content updates that happen automatically (e.g., popups, ads, page changes) can confuse users. Always give users control over such changes and provide clear cues when changes do occur.

9. **Use Accessible Media:** When including videos or audios, provide captions and transcripts. This allows users with hearing impairments to access the content and provide additional context for those who may benefit from it.

Example for a video:
```html
<video controls>
    <source src="video.mp4" type="video/mp4">
    <track src="captions.vtt" kind="subtitles" srclang="en" label="English">
    Your browser does not support the video tag.
</video>
```

10. **Test for Accessibility:** Finally, it is essential to test your website for accessibility. Use automated tools, but also conduct user testing with individuals who rely on assistive technologies to ensure your site is genuinely accessible.

Creating accessible web experiences is not simply a box to check — it is about inclusivity and honoring the diverse needs of our global audience. By embracing the principles of web accessibility and utilizing features provided by HTML5 and ARIA, developers can build websites that are usable and welcoming to everyone, regardless of their abilities. Remember, accessibility benefits not only those with disabilities but enhances the experience for all users, making the web a more inclusive space.

11. Best Practices and Coding Standards for HTML5

As web development evolves, so do the standards and practices that guide how we write HTML. Adopting best practices and coding standards not only helps in maintaining code quality but also enhances accessibility, optimization, and overall maintainability of web applications. This document outlines best practices for organizing HTML code, validating HTML5 documents, and techniques for performance optimization.

Organizing HTML Code

Organizing HTML code is crucial for readability, maintainability, and collaboration among developers. Below are some fundamental best practices:

1. **Use Semantic HTML**: Use HTML elements for their intended purpose. For example, `<header>`, `<nav>`, `<article>`, `<section>`, and `<footer>` provide

meaningful structures and improve SEO and accessibility.

```html
<header>
  <h1>My Website</h1>
  <nav>
    <ul>
      <li><a href="#home">Home</a></li>
      <li><a href="#about">About</a></li>
      <li><a href="#contact">Contact</a></li>
    </ul>
  </nav>
</header>
```

2. **Indentation and Whitespace**: Properly indent HTML elements to reflect their hierarchy clearly. This makes the code much easier to read.

```html
<article>
  <h2>Article Title</h2>
```

```html
    <p>This is a paragraph inside the article.</p>
  </article>
```

3. **Use Comments**: Use comments to section off parts of your code or explain complex sections. Avoid excessive comments, but make sure the purpose of the code is clear.

```html
<!-- Main content area -->
<main>
   <section>
      <h2>Section Heading</h2>
      <p>Content goes here...</p>
   </section>
</main>
```

4. **Consistent Naming Conventions**: When using IDs and classes, apply a naming convention such as BEM (Block Element Modifier) to ensure clarity and consistency.

```html
<div class="header__nav">
```

```
    <a href="#home" class="nav__link">Home</a>
    <a href="#about" class="nav__link">About</a>
  </div>
```

5. **Organizing Files**: Maintain a logical folder structure and file naming for your projects. A typical structure might look like:

```
/my-project
  /css
    styles.css
  /js
    script.js
  /images
  index.html
```

Validating HTML5 Documents

Validation ensures that your HTML code adheres to the standards set by W3C (World Wide Web Consortium). Here's how to validate your HTML5 documents:

1. **Use the W3C Validator**: This online tool checks your HTML and identifies errors or warnings. Just copy and paste your code or provide the URL to your web page.

   - **Link**: [W3C Markup Validation Service](https://validator.w3.org)

2. **Use Browser Developer Tools**: Most modern browsers have built-in developer tools that can help pinpoint issues within your HTML structure. You can right-click on your web page, select "Inspect", and look for errors in the console tab.

3. **Add `<!DOCTYPE html>` Declaration**: Always include the HTML5 doctype at the very top of your HTML documents to ensure browsers render your page in standards mode.

```html
<!DOCTYPE html>
<html lang="en">
<head>
    <meta charset="UTF-8">
```

```
    <meta name="viewport" content="width=device-width, initial-scale=1.0">
    <title>Document</title>
  </head>
  <body>
    ...
  </body>
</html>
```

4. **Ensure Closing Tags and Nesting**: Always close HTML tags properly and maintain the correct nesting of elements to validate your documents.

```html
<ul>
  <li>Item 1</li>
  <li>Item 2</li>
  <!-- Avoid this -->
  <li>Item 3
    <ul>
      <li>Sub Item</li>
    <!-- Incorrectly nested -->
    </ul>
  </li>
```

```
    </ul>
```

5. **Accessibility Considerations**: Use ARIA roles and attributes to enhance accessibility, especially when using custom UI elements or layouts.

```html
<button aria-label="Close" onclick="closeModal()">X</button>
```

Performance Optimization Techniques

Optimizing HTML5 documents for performance enhances user experience and can reduce load times. Here are effective techniques:

1. **Minify HTML**: Reduce file size by removing unnecessary whitespace, comments, and line breaks. Tools like HTML Minifier can automate this process.

2. **Reduce HTTP Requests**: Minimize the number of resources required to render a page.

Combine multiple CSS files into one and use image sprites where applicable.

```html
<link rel="stylesheet" href="styles/main.css">
```

3. **Optimize Images**: Use compressed image formats like JPEG 2000, WebP, or AVIF. Ensure that image dimensions in HTML match actual display sizes.

```html
<img src="images/photo.webp" alt="A beautiful scenery" width="800" height="600">
```

4. **Leverage Browser Caching**: Use cache control headers in your server configuration to instruct browsers to keep certain files cached for a specified period.

```apache
# In .htaccess
<IfModule mod_expires.c>
```

```
    ExpiresActive On
    ExpiresDefault "access plus 1 week"
    ExpiresByType image/jpg "access plus 1 month"
    ExpiresByType image/png "access plus 1 month"
    ExpiresByType image/gif "access plus 1 month"
    ExpiresByType text/css "access plus 1 week"
    ExpiresByType application/javascript "access plus 1 week"
  </IfModule>
```

5. **Defer Parsing of JavaScript**: For non-essential JavaScript, include the `defer` or `async` attribute to ensure scripts do not block HTML parsing.

```html
<script src="script.js" defer></script>
```

6. **Use Content Delivery Networks (CDNs)**: Leverage CDNs for hosting libraries and images to reduce latency and

increase load speed for your users.

7. **Responsive Design Principles**: Use viewport meta tags and CSS media queries to ensure that your website works well across various devices without unnecessary content loading.

```html
<meta name="viewport" content="width=device-width, initial-scale=1.0">
```

8. **Lazy Loading Images**: Implement lazy loading to defer loading images until they are in or near the viewport, improving initial load time.

```html
<img src="image.jpg" alt="Descriptive text" loading="lazy">
```

Implementing best practices and coding

standards when writing HTML5 is vital for ensuring that your applications are semantic, valid, maintainable, and performant. By organizing your HTML, validating it, and applying optimization techniques, you not only enhance the quality of your web pages but also improve user experience and accessibility. Following these guidelines can also help you stay aligned with the rapidly evolving web landscape, enabling you to deliver high-quality applications efficiently.

By putting these best practices into action, you will contribute to a cleaner, more organized, and more performant web ecosystem. Stay updated with trends and continue to refine your skills as new standards emerge in web development.

12. HTML5 Glossary

1. HTML5
HTML5 is the fifth and latest version of the Hypertext Markup Language (HTML), which is the standard language for creating web pages. It introduces new syntactic features, streamlined web application behavior, and multimedia elements, which enhance the multimedia capabilities of the web.

2. DOCTYPE
The `<!DOCTYPE html>` declaration should be the first line in an HTML5 document. It is used to inform the web browser about the version of HTML the page is written in. In HTML5, the declaration is simple and does not require a reference to a DTD.

Example:
```html
<!DOCTYPE html>
<html lang="en">
<head>
    <meta charset="UTF-8">
    <title>Sample Document</title>
```

```
</head>
<body>
   <h1>Welcome to HTML5</h1>
</body>
</html>
```

3. Semantic Elements
Semantic elements in HTML5 convey meaning about their contents. They help search engines and developers understand the structure of the web page, facilitating better accessibility and search optimization.

Examples:
- `<header>`: Represents introductory content or a container for navigational links.
- `<footer>`: Contains footer information for a document or section.
- `<article>`: Represents a self-contained composition in a document.
- `<section>`: Represents a thematic grouping of content.

4. Block vs. Inline Elements
HTML elements are classified as block or inline. Block elements take up the full width

available and start on a new line (e.g., `<div>`, `<p>`, `<h1>`). Inline elements occupy only the necessary width and do not start on a new line (e.g., `<span>`, `<strong>`, `<a>`).

Block Element Example:
```html
<div>
    <h2>Title</h2>
    <p>This is a block element paragraph.</p>
</div>
```

Inline Element Example:
```html
<p>This is an <strong>inline</strong> element example.</p>
```

5. Multimedia Elements
HTML5 introduced several new elements for embedding multimedia content, such as audio, video, and images.

Examples:
- `<audio>`: Used to embed sound content.

- `<video>`: Used for embedding video content.
- `<img>`: Used to embed images.

Example Usage:
```html
<video width="320" height="240" controls>
   <source src="movie.mp4" type="video/mp4">
   Your browser does not support the video tag.
</video>
```

6. Canvas
The `<canvas>` element provides a space where you can draw graphics on the fly via scripting (usually JavaScript). It is often used for rendering graphs, game graphics, and other visual images.

Example:
```html
<canvas id="myCanvas" width="200" height="100" style="border:1px solid #000000;"></canvas>
<script>
```

```
var canvas = document.getElementById("myCanvas");
var ctx = canvas.getContext("2d");
ctx.font = "30px Arial";
ctx.fillText("Hello World", 10, 50);
</script>
```

7. Form Elements
HTML5 introduced new input types and attributes, allowing for more dynamic and user-friendly forms.

New Input Types:
- `date`: For date inputs.
- `email`: For email addresses, which include validation.
- `url`: For URLs, also with validation.
- `range`: For selecting a range of numbers.

Example:
```html
<form>
    <label for="email">Email:</label>
    <input type="email" id="email" name="email"><br>
    <label for="date">Select a date:</label>
```

```html
    <input type="date" id="date"><br>
    <label for="range">Select a value:</label>
    <input type="range" id="range" min="1" max="100">
    <input type="submit">
</form>
```

8. Geolocation API
The Geolocation API allows web applications to access the geographical location of a user. It is useful for applications like maps and location-based services.

Example:
```html
<script>
function showPosition(position) {
    alert("Latitude: " + position.coords.latitude +
    ", Longitude: " + position.coords.longitude);
}

function getLocation() {
    if (navigator.geolocation) {
```

```
        navigator.geolocation.getCurrentPosition(showPosition);
    } else {
        alert("Geolocation is not supported by this browser.");
    }
}

getLocation();
</script>
```

9. Local Storage
HTML5 provides the Local Storage API, which allows for storing data in the user's browser without an expiration date. This data persists even when the browser is closed and reopened.

Example:
```html
<script>
localStorage.setItem("name", "John Doe");
let name = localStorage.getItem("name");
console.log(name); // Outputs: John Doe
</script>
```

10. Session Storage
Session Storage is similar to Local Storage but only stores data for the duration of the page session. Data stored in sessionStorage is lost when the tab is closed.

Example:
```html
<script>
sessionStorage.setItem("sessionName", "Jane Doe");
let sessionName = sessionStorage.getItem("sessionName");
console.log(sessionName); // Outputs: Jane Doe
</script>
```

11. Web Workers
Web Workers enable the execution of JavaScript scripts in background threads, allowing for concurrent processing and preventing UI interruption. This is highly beneficial for performance-intensive tasks.

Example:

```javascript
// worker.js
self.onmessage = function(e) {
    let result = e.data[0] * e.data[1];
    self.postMessage(result);
};

// main.js
let worker = new Worker('worker.js');
worker.onmessage = function(e) {
    console.log("Result: " + e.data);
};
worker.postMessage([10, 20]); // Sends data to the worker
```

12. Drag and Drop
HTML5 includes a native drag-and-drop feature that allows users to drag and drop elements between different locations on a web page.

Example:
```html
<div id="drag1" draggable="true" ondragstart="drag(event)">Drag me!</div>
<div id="div2" ondrop="drop(event)"
```

ondragover="allowDrop(event)"></div>

```
<script>
function allowDrop(ev) {
  ev.preventDefault();
}

function drag(ev) {
  ev.dataTransfer.setData("text", ev.target.id);
}

function drop(ev) {
  ev.preventDefault();
  var data = ev.dataTransfer.getData("text");

ev.target.appendChild(document.getElementById(data));
}
</script>
```

13. Microdata
HTML5 Microdata is a specification that allows for machine-readable data to be embedded within HTML documents. This is used to enhance SEO and provide structured

data for services like search engines.

Example:
```html
<div itemscope itemtype="http://schema.org/Person">
   <span itemprop="name">John Doe</span>
   <span itemprop="jobTitle">Software Engineer</span>
</div>
```

14. Web Sockets
Web Sockets provide a way for full-duplex communication channels over a single TCP connection. They allow for real-time data transfer between clients and servers.

Example:
```javascript
const socket = new WebSocket('ws://localhost:8080');
socket.onopen = function() {
   socket.send('Hello Server!');
};
socket.onmessage = function(event) {
   console.log('Message from server: ',
```

event.data);
};
```

## 15. Responsive Design

Responsive Design refers to the approach of designing web pages that adapt smoothly to different screen sizes and orientations using CSS media queries and flexible layouts.

### Example:
```css
@media screen and (max-width: 600px) {
  body {
    background-color: lightblue;
  }
}

@media screen and (min-width: 601px) {
  body {
    background-color: lightcoral;
  }
}
```

This glossary covers essential HTML5
```

elements, APIs, and concepts essential for modern web development. Understanding these terms will help you create more interactive and user-friendly web applications. Whether you're embedding multimedia, working with forms, or enhancing user experiences with new APIs, HTML5 provides the tools necessary to build responsive and powerful web applications.

Index

1. Introduction to HTML5 pg.4

2. Getting Started with HTML5 pg.14

3. Understanding HTML5 Document Structure pg.31

4. Overview of Semantic HTML pg.42

5. Understanding Text and Inline Elements in HTML pg.53

6. Images and Multimedia in HTML5 pg.63

7. Forms in HTML5 pg.81

8. Introduction to HTML5 APIs pg.92

9. Responsive Web Design in HTML5 pg.111

10. Accessibility in HTML5 pg.123

11. Best Practices and Coding Standards for HTML5 pg.135

12. HTML5 Glossary pg.146

www.ingramcontent.com/pod-product-compliance
Lightning Source LLC
Chambersburg PA
CBHW052205220526
45471CB00004B/1819